★ ★

FRONTIERSMEN OF AMERICA

Davy Crockett

FRONTIER ADVENTURER

MATTHEW G. GRANT

Illustrated by Jack Norman

GALLERY OF GREAT AMERICANS SERIES

★ ★

Davy Crockett

FRONTIER ADVENTURER

Text copyright © 1974 by Publication Associates. Illustrations copyright © 1974 by Creative Education. International copyrights reserved in all countries. No part of this book may be reproduced in any form without written permission from the publisher. Printed in the United States.

Library of Congress Number: 73-10072   ISBN: O-87191-258-9

Published by Creative Education, Mankato, Minnesota 56001

Library of Congress Cataloging in Publication Data
Grant, Matthew G.
  Davy Crockett—frontier adventure.
                    (Gallery of great Americans)
  SUMMARY: A brief biography of the Tennessee woodsman renowned as a hunter, scout, politician, and soldier.
  1. Crockett, David, 1786-1836—Juvenile literature. [1. Crockett, David, 1786-1836. 2. Frontier and pioneer life] I. Title. F436.C9515 976.8'04'0924 [B] [92] 73-10072 ISBN 0-87191-258-9

CONTENTS

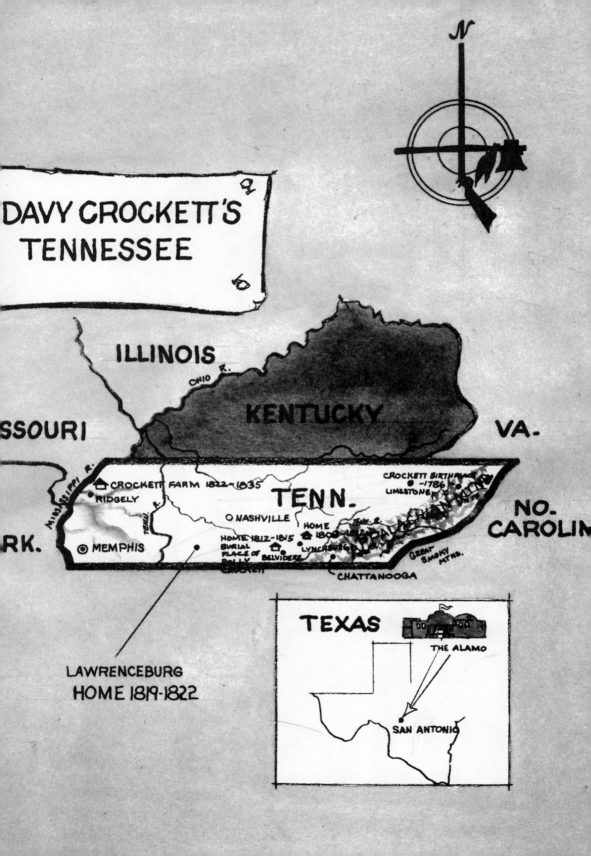

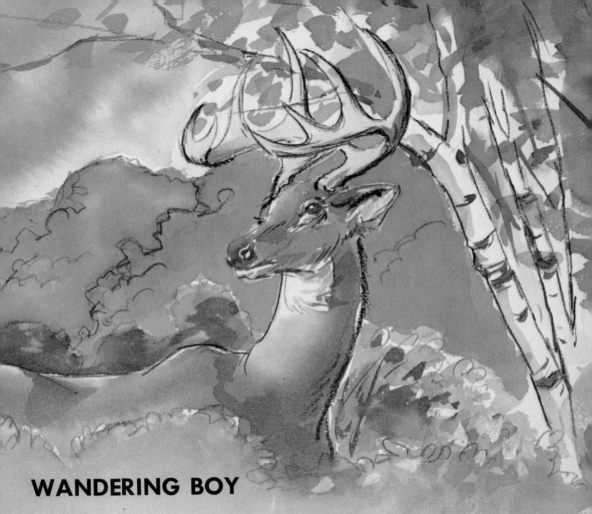

WANDERING BOY

From the time he was eight, Davy Crockett had to hunt for meat. His father gave him a flintlock and said: "Here's one ball and one charge. Bring back meat or you get no supper."

It was hard on the boy. But the Crockett family was desperately poor. They lived in the backwoods of eastern Tennessee. Mr. Crockett had tried being a farmer and a miller and had failed. Then he opened a small inn.

When Davy was 12, his father hired him out to a passing traveler. The man needed a herd-boy to help with his cattle. He was going to Virginia.

Davy walked 400 miles, prodding cows all the way. Then he talked some kindly wagon-drivers into bringing him home.

His father sent him to school. But Davy only got into trouble and soon ran away. He hired out to another cattleman and started wandering all over Virginia and Maryland, taking odd jobs when he could. When he had no job, he roamed the woods.

After two footloose years he came home and did farm work to help pay the family's debts. But the wandering spirit was still in him and it would be there until the day he died.

In 1804, when he was 18, he married Polly Finley. He tried farming for awhile, but what he really loved was hunting. He was the best shot in the whole area—and everybody knew it.

The Crocketts had two children. Then Davy's wandering itch took over and he moved his family westward to the Elk River. It was wild country, the kind Davy liked best. Inside of a year, he had killed 105 bears. People began to tell tall tales about his hunting abilities.

Ever restless, he moved his family again. Then word came that the Creek Indians were at war.

13

THE INDIAN-FIGHTER

General Andrew Jackson was raising an army to fight the Creeks. Davy volunteered almost at once to be a scout. Polly wept and begged him not to go, but his mind was made up.

The Creek Indians had been stirred to war by the great Indian leader, Tecumseh. They feared that the whites would soon drive them from their homeland. It was a fear that came true only too soon.

Andrew Jackson hated the Indians. But his chief scout, Davy Crockett, came to admire them even as he fought them. The Creeks were only fighting for their homes. Davy could understand that.

Davy fought in Alabama and Georgia. The army was often short of food and the men welcomed the wild game Davy brought in.

Davy and some men went south into Florida and fought the Indians there. Then the war ended. Davy was glad. "I never liked this business with the Indians," he said later. He went home to Polly and took up his farmer's life once more.

CONGRESSMAN CROCKETT

For a few years he was happy. Then Polly died. Davy was left with two small sons and a baby girl. After a time he married Elizabeth Patton, a widow with two children whose husband had died in the war.

Now the old restless feeling laid hold
of Davy again. He moved from place to
place—never satisfied. About 1822 he went
to far western Tennessee. There, near the

Mississippi river, he settled down near Reelfoot Lake. It was a lonely, mysterious land. The lake itself had been created by a monstrous earthquake in 1811. Sometimes the ground still trembled as Davy planted corn.

If there was anything Davy loved better than hunting, it was telling tall tales and funny stories. In those days, when there were no radios or television and even newspapers were rare, a story-teller was a valued citizen. And the neighbors knew Davy not only as a man with a glib tongue, but also as a war hero and "the best bear hunter in the West."

So they nominated him to the legislature.

He served the people well when he was elected. And he continued to tell the funny backwoods tales that were his trademark. His fame spread even beyond Tennessee. Soon people began to talk about sending him to Congress in Washington.

In 1827, when the next election was held, David Crockett was elected Representative from the district of western Tennessee.

People called him the "Coonskin Con-gressman," even though he wore ordinary clothes. But nothing could hide his pioneer shrewdness, his honesty, nor his ability to smell out a phony. Up to this time, most congressmen had been wealthy and educated men. But Crockett was a man of the people who proved he could beat seasoned politicians at their own game.

He was re-elected for a second term.

He fought for the rights of small home-steaders, who were being driven from their lands by rich men. He became a champion of the southeastern Indians, who were driven

from their lands by the whites. President Jackson, who had been Crockett's friend, turned
against him. Crockett's bills on behalf of the
poor farmers and the Indians were defeated
He himself lost the election in 1831.

HERO OF THE ALAMO

He made a brief return to Congress in 1833. But his continued fighting on behalf of the Indians made him many enemies. He tried for re-election in 1835 and was defeated.

"If Tennessee doesn't want me, I'll go to Texas!" he exclaimed. Leaving his family to follow later, he set off for this remote place. It was then a part of Mexico.

He arrived in the middle of a new war.

English-speaking Texans had decided to break free of Mexico and form a republic. Mexico sent a large army to punish the Texas rebels.

At that time, early in 1836, only one fort stood in the path of the Mexican army. It was the old Alamo mission at San Antonio. Crockett hurried to join in its defense. He was welcomed by William Travis, its young commander, and Jim Bowie, a famous adventurer.

On February 22, 1836, an army of about 3,000 Mexican troops surrounded the little fort.

Davy Crockett and the other 186 defenders of the Alamo held out for 12 days, hoping that reinforcements would soon arrive. On the morning of March 6 the Mexican army stormed the Alamo walls. Fighting hand to hand, the Alamo defenders died to the last man. Their bodies were burned by the Mexicans.

"Remember the Alamo!" The cry rang out all over Texas. A few weeks later, the republic was free.

GALLERY OF GREAT AMERICANS SERIES

INDIANS OF AMERICA
GERONIMO
CRAZY HORSE
CHIEF JOSEPH
PONTIAC
SQUANTO
OSCEOLA

EXPLORERS OF AMERICA
COLUMBUS
LEIF ERICSON
DeSOTO
LEWIS AND CLARK
CHAMPLAIN
CORONADO

FRONTIERSMEN OF AMERICA
DANIEL BOONE
BUFFALO BILL
JIM BRIDGER
FRANCIS MARION
DAVY CROCKETT
KIT CARSON

WAR HEROES OF AMERICA
JOHN PAUL JONES
PAUL REVERE
ROBERT E. LEE
ULYSSES S. GRANT
SAM HOUSTON
LAFAYETTE

WOMEN OF AMERICA
CLARA BARTON
JANE ADDAMS
ELIZABETH BLACKWELL
HARRIET TUBMAN
SUSAN B. ANTHONY
DOLLEY MADISON